My First Book about Crocodilian

Amazing Animal Books
Children's Picture Books

By Molly Davidson

Mendon Cottage Books

JD-Biz Publishing

Read More Amazing Animal Books

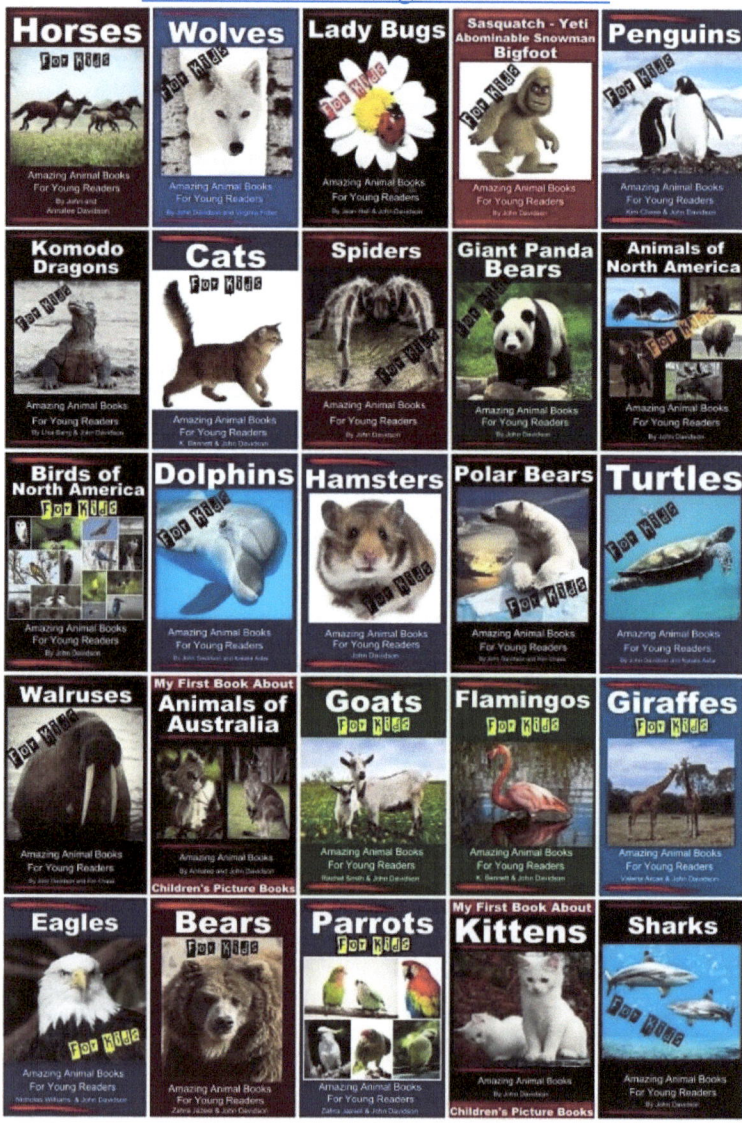

Table of Contents

Introduction

The crocodilian family includes alligators, caimans, gharial, false gharial, and of course, crocodiles.

Crocodilian have been around for millions of years, back to the prehistoric ages.

They have very powerful jaws and are quick in the water, making them a very dangerous reptile.

What is a crocodilian?

Crocodilian are some of the largest reptiles in the World, they live both on land and in the water.

An alligator

They can grow be up to 20 feet long, also have very long snouts full of sharp teeth.

Crocodilians have their eyes and nose on the tops of their heads; this is so they can hide in the water.

Crocodilians are coldblooded, meaning they need outside heat to keep them warm; this is why they like to lay in the sun.

They are very fast swimmers, but not as fast on land. If you are trying to run away from a crocodilian run in a zigzag pattern, they cannot turn very well.

They can bite down with great strength, but they don't have much strength in opening their mouths.

What kinds of crocodilians are there?

There are the largest numbers of alligator and crocodile species, but there are a few caiman, gharial, and false gharials too.

There are about 9 species of crocodiles, and then there are species of American and Chinese alligators.

Where do crocodilians live?

Crocodilian live in warm climates, usually tropical; they would not survive in Antarctica.

The Nile crocodile is a very large species, which lives in Egypt and is known for attaching humans.

The Chinese alligator lives in Asia, but it fairly small and endangered.

Crocodilians are also found in most zoos, but the zoos in colder climates will keep them inside during the winter.

The history of crocodilians and humans

The ancient Egyptians knew the power of the Nile crocodile, even one of their gods had a crocodile's head.

Around the 1960's in the U.S. places called alligator farms were started. Alligators were grown, cared for, and taught tricks; tourists were able to come watch.

A baby crocodile in a human's hands

Slowly the farms started selling the alligators skin, which was then used for boots, purses, and belts

Over the years some people have tried to keep crocodilian as pets, they are fine when they are tiny babies, but then they grow up and get too big.

Not all species of species of crocodilian will attack humans, crocodilian usually just strike if it is an easy food target.

How do crocodilians act?

All crocodilian are carnivores, meaning meat eaters.

Gharilas usually eat fish, but the Chinese alligator eats shell fish.

The American alligator and several others will eat just about any meat they can catch.

They will spend most of their time in the water; this is where they do their hunting

After the crocodilian mate, the mother will go lay her eggs on land, in a hidden nest. She will keep a close watch on her eggs, so other animals will not eat them.

After the babies hatch most crocodilian mothers leave their babies to survive on their own, but some will keep them close for about a year or two.

From the time the crocodilian is in the egg until it becomes an adult, they will talk to other, using yelping noises mostly.

Adults usually bellow or roar at each other to talk.

Nile crocodiles

The Nile crocodile is the second largest crocodile and is found all over Africa.

They like to live in brackism lakes, marshes, rivers, and sometimes the ocean.

Nile crocodiles will wait in one place for hours, days, even weeks, to try to get the perfect kill.

They are so quick and have such strong jaws, small animals are usually crushed with one bite, and larger animals may have to be drug under the water and drowned.

Nile crocodiles like to live in large groups; they also will share food with each other.

The oldest and biggest Nile crocodile is the leader of the group.

They kill more humans per year than sharks do; humans are just easy targets for the huge crocodile.

Their skin is very thick and scaly, like armor, but their scales do not overlap like other animals.

Many years ago, the Nile crocodile was endangered because so many people wanted their skin.

Alligators

There are two types of alligators; the Chinese and the American alligator.

A Chinese alligator floating in the water

American alligators can be found in the U.S. in Louisiana and Florida, also in Mississippi, Alabama, North and South Carolina.

Many tourists come to the southern United States to take a boat tour to see alligators.

Boy American alligators like to stay by themselves, but in the same territory as others.

The American alligator is about 6 feet longer than the Chinese alligator.

Chinese alligators are endangered, there are less than 100 left in the wild.

Alligators like to eat their food in one bite. If it is too big to fit they will roll it around to break it off until it will fit inside their mouths.

They do not usually attack humans, they just leave the area.

Mother alligators will make their nests in weeds or warm sand, this helps keep the eggs warm.

The temperature of the nest determines if the alligators are all girls, lower temperature, or boys, a higher temperature.

All the eggs in the same nest will be the same gender.

The number one killer of baby alligators is adult alligators; they will sometimes eat their babies as a snack.

Caiman

Caimens are in the same group as alligators, they just live in Central and South America.

Spectacled caiman

The spectacled caiman, also called the white caiman, is the most common crocodilian in the World.

They have wider and shorter snouts than alligators and crocodiles.

Most caimans eat snails and fish, some do eat wild pigs.

Mother caimans will try to build the biggest nest possible for her eggs.

Baby caimans will stay with their mothers for the first two to four months after hatching.

Caimans are not known to attack humans; usually the only time they will attack is if a mother sees a human messing with her eggs.

Gharial

The gharial is also called a fish-eating crocodile, and they live mostly in India

They have long, thin snouts that they turn sideways to catch fish, tadpoles, and to crush open crustacean shells, like crabs.

A gharial in a zoo

The gharial is the longest of all the crocodialian, they grow to be about 20 feet long!

They live mostly in rivers, the problem is there are many people in India, and so they are taking over the gharials' habitat, making them endangered.

False gharial

A false gharial is a cousin to the gharial from India, they live in Malaysia and Sumatra.

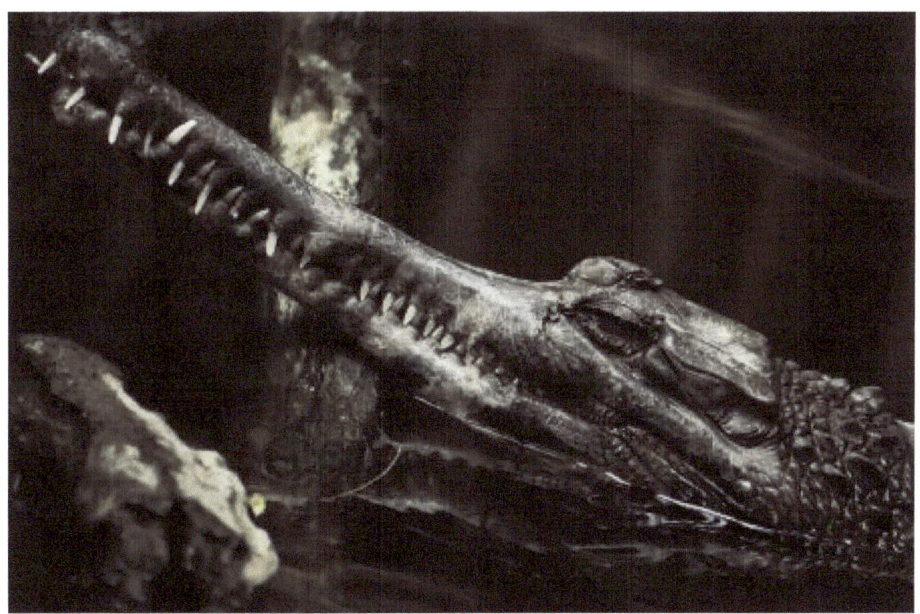

A false gharial

They will basically eat anything they can, like monkeys, deer, and macaques.

Mothers will lay their eggs in a nest, and won't ever come back for her babies; they have to survive on their own from the day they hatch.

Just like gharials, false gharials are becoming endangered, because people are draining the swamps that they live in.

Conclusion

Crocodilian are some of the world's biggest reptiles, and because of this they are usually one of the top predators in their area.

Publisher

JD-Biz Corp

P O Box 374

Mendon, Utah 84325

http://www.jd-biz.com/